Raising Emotionally Tough Boys and Girls

A Parent's Handbook for Nurturing Resilient, and Emotionally Strong Kids

+ 30 DAYS EFFECTIVE PARENTING PLAN

By

Jennifer A. Mickens

Copyright

Copyright © 2024 by Jennifer A. Mickens

Dedication

To all the parents who tirelessly nurture and support their children's journey, may your love and guidance inspire them to reach for the stars and embrace the strength within their hearts.

Table of Contents

Contents

My Turbulent Parenting Journey with My Daughter Emily

Amidst the tempest of motherhood, I navigate the tumultuous seas of parenting alongside my daughter Emily, a journey fraught with unexpected challenges and poignant lessons!

In the maze of parenthood, my journey with my daughter Emily stands out as a beacon of resilience and unwavering love. From the very beginning, Emily's presence in my life was like a whirlwind, challenging me in ways I never anticipated. But it was through facing these challenges head-on that I discovered the true depth of my strength as a mother.

Emily was born with a spirit as fierce as a lion's roar and a will as unyielding as the mountains. Her determination was evident from the moment she took her first breath, and as she grew, so did the intensity of her spirit. But with her fierce determination came a set of challenges that tested me in ways I never imagined.

I vividly recall the countless nights spent pacing the floor, cradling Emily in my arms as tears streamed down both our faces. It seemed that no matter what I did, I couldn't ease her frustration or soothe her restless spirit. In those moments of despair, I questioned my abilities as a mother, wondering if I was equipped to handle the challenges that lay ahead.

But it was during those darkest moments that I found my greatest source of strength – Emily herself. Despite the challenges she faced, Emily approached each day with courage and resilience that left me in awe. Her unwavering determination to overcome every obstacle in her path inspired me to dig deep and find the strength within myself to keep going. It was through navigating the complexities of parenting Emily that the idea for this book was born. I wanted to create a resource that not only shared my experiences but also offered guidance and support to other parents facing similar challenges. I knew firsthand the struggles and frustrations that came with nurturing a strong-willed child, and I wanted to offer a beacon of hope to parents who felt lost in the tumult of parenthood.

The pages of this book are a testament to the resilience and strength that lies within every parent. From understanding emotional toughness to navigating challenges and prioritizing self-care, every word is a reflection of the lessons learned from my journey with Emily. I hope that by sharing our story, other parents will find solace, inspiration, and practical guidance as they navigate the highs and lows of parenthood.

As I look back on the journey that brought me to this moment, I am filled with gratitude for the opportunity to share our story with the world. May our journey serve as a beacon of hope for parents everywhere, and may the lessons learned along the way continue to shape our journeys as parents for years to come.

Introduction

Unleashing the Strength within Your Child

Welcome to "Strength in Heart: A Parent's Handbook for Raising Resilient, and Emotionally Strong Kids," where we embark on a transformative journey to unlock the hidden potential within every child. Parenting isn't just about raising children; it's about nurturing resilient, compassionate individuals who can conquer life's challenges with grace and determination.

A few years ago, I lived in the same compound with a single mother raising her son in the bustling city of New York. Like many parents, she faced her fair share of challenges, but none as daunting as when her son, then 10 years old, experienced relentless bullying at school. Despite her best efforts to console him, she watched helplessly as his confidence plummeted, and his once vibrant spirit began to fade. It was during this dark period that she stumbled upon the concept of emotional toughness and the power it holds in shaping a child's resilience. With newfound determination, she immersed herself in learning everything she could about nurturing emotional strength in children.

Through tireless dedication and unwavering love, she implemented the strategies outlined in "Strength in Heart." She created a safe space for her son to express his feelings openly, validated his emotions, and equipped him with practical coping mechanisms to navigate the challenges he faced. Slowly but surely, she witnessed a remarkable transformation in her son. He began to stand a little taller, speak a little louder, and face each day with renewed confidence and resilience. The once timid boy who avoided confrontation now faced his bullies head-on, armed with the inner strength and courage instilled in him by his devoted mother.

Inspired by her son's journey, she realized the profound impact that nurturing emotional toughness can have on a child's life. It wasn't just about weathering storms; it was about emerging from them stronger, more resilient, and more compassionate than ever before.

Within the pages of this handbook, you'll discover a treasure trove of insights, strategies, and practical tools to guide you on this empowering journey. Each chapter is crafted to inspire and empower you as you navigate parenthood's beautiful, yet sometimes daunting, terrain, with several Positive Affirmations to help you and your child in the parenting journey

As you delve into this handbook, I invite you to embark on a voyage of self-discovery and growth alongside your child. Embrace each chapter as an opportunity to deepen your connection, strengthen your bond, and unlock the limitless potential that resides within both you and your child. Together, let's ignite the flame of resilience in the hearts of our children, empowering them to navigate life's twists and turns with courage, grace, and unwavering heart. The journey ahead may be challenging, but the rewards are immeasurable.

Thank you for entrusting me to be your guide on this extraordinary adventure. Let's embark on this journey together, and together, let's change the world—one resilient heart at a time.

Chapter One

Understanding Emotional Toughness

What is Emotional Toughness?

In the journey of parenting, few qualities are as vital as emotional toughness. But what exactly does it mean to be emotionally tough, especially for children?

I've known a young girl, who loves to draw and dreams of becoming an artist one day. The girl faces a challenge when her classmates tease her about her drawings, calling her "weird" and "strange." Despite feeling hurt and discouraged, she did not give up on her passion. Instead, she takes a deep breath, brushes off the negative comments, and continues to pursue her love for art.

This is a perfect example of emotional toughness in action. Emotional toughness is like an invisible shield that helps children like the girl face difficult situations and keep moving forward. It's the strength inside them that allows them to bounce back from setbacks, stay positive in tough times, and believe in themselves no matter what. Emotional toughness is the inner resilience that allows individuals to navigate life's challenges with courage, strength, and adaptability. It's more than just having a thick skin or suppressing emotions; it's about facing adversity head-on, embracing setbacks as opportunities for growth, and emerging stronger on the other side.

For children, emotional toughness manifests as the ability to bounce back from disappointments, handle stress and adversity effectively, and maintain a positive outlook even in the face of adversity. It's about developing a resilient mindset that enables them to persevere through life's ups and downs with grace and determination.

At its core, emotional toughness involves several key characteristics and traits. These include;

Resilience: This is a lifestyle that empowers children to recover quickly from setbacks and difficulties,

Adaptability: This attribute enables them to adjust to change and adversity

Perseverance: This attribute empowers the kids to stay the course even when faced with challenges. I call these traits **The "RAP" Medicine**.

Contrary to popular belief, emotional toughness is not about being stoic or unfeeling. It's quite the opposite. Emotionally tough individuals are in touch with their emotions and can express them in healthy and constructive ways. They understand that experiencing emotions is a natural part of being human and that vulnerability is not a sign of weakness but of strength.

In today's fast-paced and ever-changing world, the need for emotional toughness has never been greater. Children are faced with a myriad of challenges, from academic pressure and social media stress to family upheavals and global crises. By equipping them with the tools and mindset of emotional toughness, you can empower your children to thrive in the face of adversity and emerge as resilient, compassionate, and confident individuals.

Misconceptions and Myths Surrounding Emotional Toughness

- **Emotional toughness means suppressing emotions:** Contrary to this belief, emotional toughness is not about ignoring or suppressing emotions. It's about acknowledging and understanding emotions while developing the resilience to cope with them effectively.

- **Emotionally tough kids don't need support:** Some may mistakenly think that emotionally tough kids can handle everything on their own. In reality, even emotionally resilient children benefit from supportive relationships and guidance from trusted adults.

- **Emotional toughness is the same as being "tough" or "hard":** Emotional toughness is often misunderstood as being unemotional or indifferent. In truth, emotionally tough kids are sensitive to their feelings and the feelings of others, but they have developed healthy coping mechanisms to manage emotions in challenging situations.

- **Emotionally tough kids don't experience stress or anxiety:** While emotionally tough kids may be better equipped to handle stress and adversity, they are not immune to these feelings. They may still experience stress, anxiety, or other difficult emotions, but they have learned how to cope with them constructively.

- **Emotional toughness is innate and cannot be developed:** Some believe that emotional toughness is something you're either born with or without. In reality, emotional toughness is a skill that can be nurtured and developed over time through practice, experience, and supportive relationships.

The Role of Emotional Intelligence in Child Development

Emotional intelligence, or EQ, is like a superpower that helps children understand and manage their emotions, navigate social situations, and build strong relationships. Imagine a classroom where students are working on a group project. One student, Emily, is feeling nervous about presenting her ideas to the class. Sensing Emily's unease, Jacob offers her words of encouragement and helps her brainstorm ideas for the presentation. His empathy and ability to understand Emily's feelings not only ease her anxiety but also strengthen their bond as friends. That is the work of Emotional Intelligence.

But what exactly is emotional intelligence, and how does it work? Emotional intelligence consists of four key components: self-awareness, self-regulation, social awareness, and relationship management.

1. **Self-awareness** is the ability to recognize and understand one's own emotions. It's about being in tune with how you feel and why you feel that way. For instance, recognizing when someone is feeling happy, sad, or frustrated and understanding the reasons behind those emotions.

2. **Self-regulation** is the ability to control and manage one's emotions, thoughts, and behaviors. It's about staying calm under pressure, resisting impulses, and thinking before acting.

3. **Social awareness** is the ability to understand and empathize with the emotions of others. It's about recognizing when someone is happy, sad, or upset and showing compassion and support.

4. **Relationship management** is the ability to build and maintain healthy relationships with others. It's about communicating effectively, resolving conflicts, and working collaboratively towards shared goals. A child excels in relationship management by fostering positive connections

with his/her peers and showing respect and kindness to everyone he/she meets.

Imagine a world without emotional intelligence!

As parents, we often focus on our children's academic success and physical well-being, but one equally important aspect, yet sometimes overlooked, is their emotional intelligence. Emotional intelligence plays a crucial role in shaping children's lives and future success in various aspects. Here's why it's so significant:

Children develop strong interpersonal skills, such as empathy, communication, and conflict resolution. These skills are essential for forming and maintaining healthy relationships with family members, friends, teachers, and peers. By understanding and managing their own emotions and recognizing the emotions of others, children can build meaningful connections and navigate social situations with confidence. Research has shown that emotional intelligence is strongly correlated with academic success. Children with higher levels of emotional intelligence tend to perform better in school, have higher grades, and exhibit better behavior in the classroom. This is because emotional intelligence helps children manage stress, stay focused, and engage in effective problem-solving, all of which are essential skills for academic success.

Inevitably, children will face challenges and setbacks throughout their lives. Emotional intelligence equips them with the resilience and coping skills needed to navigate these challenges effectively. Adopting a positive mindset, regulating their reactions, and understanding their emotions will help children bounce back from adversity, learn from their experiences, and grow stronger in the process.

One significant aspect of children is mental well-being. Emotional intelligence is closely linked to mental health and overall well-being. Moreover, children who are tough emotionally are better equipped to manage stress, anxiety, and other negative emotions. They are also more likely to have higher self-esteem, better self-confidence, and a greater sense of self-worth. As parents or aspiring parents, we can prioritize emotional intelligence in parenting lifestyle, we can help foster mental and emotional resilience in our children, setting them on a path to lifelong well-being. Meanwhile, beyond academic and social success, emotional intelligence lays the foundation for essential life skills such as leadership, decision-making, and adaptability. By enhancing their emotional intelligence, children learn to navigate the complexities of the world with confidence, integrity, and empathy. These skills are invaluable in both personal and professional contexts and will serve them well throughout their lives.

One of the most valuable things we can teach our kids as they navigate parenting is how to overcome setbacks with perseverance and resilience. These are some doable tactics I've used over the years to foster resilience in children, which have proven effective in my parenting journey:

1. Cultivate a Growth Mindset

Consider your child confronted with a complex math problem that seems impossible at first glance. Instead of succumbing to frustration, they draw upon your shared teachings about the value of hard work and persistence. This mindset shift allows them to approach the problem with determination rather than defeatism. As they persevere through the challenge, you, as a parent, offer praise for the correct answers and their dedication and resilience in tackling the problem. This acknowledgment reinforces the idea that their efforts matter as much as if not more than, the outcome itself. It cultivates a belief within them that they possess the capability to overcome hurdles through their perseverance and determination.

This cycle of facing challenges, exerting effort, and receiving recognition for their resilience builds a sense of self-assurance in your child. They begin to understand that setbacks are not roadblocks, but rather opportunities for growth and learning. With each obstacle overcome, they become more confident in their ability to navigate future challenges, knowing that their perseverance will ultimately lead to success.

2. Foster Independence and Problem-Solving Skills

Consider a young student who is faced with an issue at school. Rather than jumping in to solve the problem immediately, you encourage the youngster to come up with several solutions on their own. Through this process, the child gains the ability to solve problems independently, increasing their independence and preparing them for challenges later in life. A child gains confidence when they are encouraged to solve problems independently. They become less dependent on other people for answers and begin to have confidence in their skills. They feel more confident and can take on issues head-on because they believe they have what it takes to go through them. The youngster gains important resilience lessons as they discuss and investigate possible alternatives. They understand that setbacks are a natural part of problem-solving and use these experiences to grow stronger and more adaptable. This approach teaches them that failure is not the end but an opportunity to learn and improve.

3. Provide a Safe and Supportive Environment

Imagine a situation when a child brings up a school project during a family get-together at the dinner table. Rather than dismissing her concerns, the family listens intently and offers consolation. The youngster can feel safe and accepted in this loving setting, which gives them a sense of love and support. The child gains resiliency skills in this cozy environment. With her family's support, she feels more equipped to take on challenges head-on. As a result, she learns resilience from this event, which helps her overcome setbacks and hurdles. By creating a secure and nurturing home, the family gives the child the emotional resilience to deal with life's ups and downs. This base of acceptance and affection gives her the conviction that she can overcome any challenge that comes her way, ultimately helping her succeed both academically and personally.

4. Encourage healthy Coping Mechanisms

Equip your child with effective coping strategies, teaching them techniques such as deep breathing exercises and positive self-talk providing them with the tools to manage their emotions constructively, fostering resilience in the face of adversity.

5. Lead by Example

As a parent, your actions speak louder than words. When you face setbacks, demonstrate perseverance and adaptability. Your children observe how you handle challenges, and by sharing your experiences of overcoming obstacles, you inspire them to cultivate resilience in their own lives.

6. Celebrate Successes and Milestones

Recognizing and celebrating your child's achievements, whether big or small, is crucial for building resilience and self-confidence. Through acknowledgment of their successes at school and praising their efforts, you reinforce their belief in their abilities and resilience to tackle future challenges.

7. Foster a Sense of Purpose and Meaning

Encouraging your child to explore their interests and passions helps your child discover strengths and values through sincere support, you help them find purpose and meaning in pursuing their goals. This sense of direction empowers them to face life's challenges with determination and resilience.

Positive Affirmations for Building Resilience and Confidence for Your Kid

"I am strong, and I can overcome any challenge that comes my way."

"I believe in myself and my abilities to handle difficult situations."

"Mistakes help me grow, and I am always learning and improving."

"I am resilient, and I bounce back from setbacks with determination."

"I am capable of handling my emotions in a healthy and constructive way."

"I am surrounded by love and support from my family and friends."

"I am unique and special just the way I am."

"I have the power to make a positive difference in the world."

"I am brave, and I face my fears with courage."

"I am smart, and I can figure out solutions to any problem."

"I am worthy of love, respect, and kindness."

"I am kind and compassionate towards myself and others."

"I am patient, and I trust that everything happens for a reason."

"I am capable of achieving my goals with hard work and perseverance."

"I am grateful for all the blessings in my life, and I embrace each day with positivity and gratitude.

Chapter Two

Strategies for Raising Emotionally Tough Kids

Creating a Supportive Home Environment

✔ **Establishing Routines:**

Routines are like the backbone of a child's day-to-day life. They provide structure and predictability, which are crucial for a child's sense of security. From waking up at the same time each morning to having regular meal times and bedtime rituals, routines help children know what to expect and feel a sense of control over their environment. Consistent routines also help regulate biological processes like sleep-wake cycles, which contribute to overall well-being. Parents can customize routines to fit their family's needs, incorporating activities that promote bonding and quality time together.

• Identify Priorities: Determine the most important daily activities for your child's well-being, such as sleep, meals, play, and learning.

- Create a Schedule: Develop a consistent daily schedule that includes regular times for waking up, meals, naps (if applicable), playtime, learning activities, and bedtime.

- Communicate Expectations: Communicate the daily routine to your child using visual aids like charts or diagrams, especially for younger children who may not yet grasp the concept of time.

- Lead by Example: Model the behaviors you want to see in your child by following the same routines yourself, demonstrating the importance of consistency and structure.

- Be Flexible: While routines provide stability, it's essential to remain flexible and adapt to changes or unexpected events without causing undue stress for you or your child.

✔ **Creating Physical Space:**

The physical environment of the home plays a significant role in shaping children's behavior and emotions. Designating specific areas for different activities, such as a quiet corner for reading or a space for creative play, helps children develop a sense of order and purpose. A clutter-free environment reduces distractions and allows children to focus on their tasks and interests. Moreover, involving children in the organization and decoration of their space empowers them and fosters a sense of ownership and responsibility.

• Designate Zones: Allocate specific areas within your home for different activities, such as a play area, study corner, relaxation space, and communal areas for family gatherings.

• Declutter Regularly: Set aside time to declutter and organize each area of your home, involving your child in the process to teach them organization skills and foster a sense of ownership.

• Personalize the Space: Allow your child to personalize their designated areas with their favorite toys, books, artwork, or decorations, creating a sense of belonging and identity.

• Safety First: Ensure that the physical environment is safe and child-friendly by securing furniture, covering electrical outlets, and removing any hazards that could pose a risk to your child's well-being.

• Create Boundaries: Establish clear boundaries for each area of the home, setting expectations for how they should be used and respected by all family members.

✔ **Encouraging Open Communication:**

Effective communication is the cornerstone of a healthy family dynamic. Parents should strive to create an environment where children feel comfortable expressing their thoughts, feelings, and concerns without fear of judgment or retribution. Active listening, empathy, and validation are essential skills that parents can cultivate to strengthen their connection with their children. By engaging in open dialogue, parents gain insight into their children's experiences and perspectives, which helps foster trust and mutual respect.

•   Be Approachable: Foster an environment where your child feels comfortable approaching you with any questions, concerns, or thoughts they may have, without fear of judgment or criticism.

•   Practice Active Listening: Listen attentively to your child's words, thoughts, and feelings, giving them your full attention and demonstrating empathy and understanding.

•   Validate Emotions: Acknowledge and validate your child's feelings, even if you don't necessarily agree with them, to show that their emotions are valued and respected.

•   Use Age-Appropriate Language: Tailor your communication style to your child's age and developmental level, using simple language and concepts that they can understand.

•   Set Aside Quality Time: Dedicate regular one-on-one time with your child to engage in meaningful conversations, activities, or shared interests, strengthening your bond and fostering trust.

✔ **Cultivating Emotional Intelligence:**

Emotional intelligence refers to the ability to recognize, understand, and manage one's emotions, as well as to empathize with others.

Parents can support their children's emotional development by acknowledging and validating their feelings, even if they may seem trivial or irrational. Teaching children to identify and express their emotions in healthy ways helps them develop self-awareness and emotional resilience. Additionally, parents can model empathy, problem-solving, and conflict-resolution skills, which are essential components of emotional intelligence.

• Label Emotions: Help your child identify and label their emotions by using descriptive language and providing examples of different feelings.

• Teach Coping Strategies: Teach your child healthy coping strategies for managing difficult emotions, such as deep breathing, mindfulness exercises, or engaging in favorite activities.

• Model Emotional Regulation: Demonstrate healthy ways of expressing and regulating your own emotions, serving as a positive role model for your child to emulate.

• Encourage Empathy: Foster empathy in your child by encouraging them to consider others' perspectives and feelings, and by praising acts of kindness and compassion.

• Problem-Solve Together: Involve your child in problem-solving discussions to help them develop critical thinking skills and learn how to resolve conflicts or challenges constructively.

✔ **Promoting Positive Discipline:**

Positive discipline focuses on teaching and guiding children towards responsible behavior rather than punishing them for mistakes or misbehavior. It emphasizes communication, respect, and problem-solving rather than coercion or punishment. Parents can set clear expectations and boundaries for behavior, and provide consistent consequences that are logical and age-appropriate. Positive reinforcement, such as praise and encouragement, helps reinforce desirable behaviors and fosters a positive parent-child relationship based on mutual respect and understanding.

• Set Clear Expectations: Establish clear rules and expectations for behavior, outlining the consequences of both positive and negative actions in advance.

• Use Positive Reinforcement: Praise and reward your child for demonstrating desired behaviors, using specific and sincere praise to reinforce their efforts.

• Redirect Misbehavior: Instead of focusing on punishment, redirect your child's attention and energy towards more appropriate behaviors or activities.

• Teach Problem-Solving Skills: Encourage your child to actively participate in finding solutions to problems or conflicts, promoting independence and self-reliance.

• Stay Calm and Consistent: Maintain a calm and composed demeanor when addressing misbehavior, and apply consequences consistently and fairly to reinforce the importance of accountability and respect.

✔ **Fostering a Sense of Belonging:**

Children thrive when they feel connected and valued within their family unit. Parents can foster a sense of belonging by creating rituals, traditions, and routines that strengthen family bonds. These could include regular family meals, game nights, or holiday traditions that create shared experiences and memories. Involving children in decision-making and problem-solving within the family reinforces their sense of agency and belonging, helping them feel valued and respected as contributing members of the family.

Teaching Problem-Solving Skills

✔ **Identify the Problem:**

Teaching children to identify and define the problem is the first step toward finding a solution. Encourage them to articulate their concerns or challenges they are facing. By breaking down complex issues into smaller, more manageable parts, children gain clarity and understanding of the problem at hand. Parents can facilitate this process by asking open-ended questions and actively listening to their child's perspective.

✔ Brainstorm Solutions:

Once the problem is identified, encourage children to brainstorm potential solutions. Emphasize that every idea is valuable, regardless of how unconventional it might appear. This fosters creativity and encourages children to think outside the box. Parents can facilitate brainstorming sessions by offering prompts or suggestions to get the creative juices flowing. Encourage children to consider multiple perspectives and explore a variety of options.

✔ Evaluate and Choose Solutions:

After generating a list of potential solutions, help children evaluate each option. Discuss the pros and cons of each solution, considering factors such as feasibility, effectiveness, and potential consequences. Encourage children to think critically and weigh the potential outcomes of each choice. Guide them in making an informed decision by considering their values, preferences, and goals. Ultimately, empowers children to choose a solution they believe in and are willing to implement.

✔ Implement and Reflect:

Once a solution is chosen, support children in implementing their decision. Provide guidance and assistance as needed, but encourage children to take ownership of the process. Afterward, facilitate a reflection on the outcome. Encourage children to evaluate the effectiveness of their chosen solution, considering what worked well and what could be improved upon. Discuss any unexpected challenges or outcomes, and help children extract valuable lessons from their experience. This reflection process reinforces learning and encourages continuous improvement in problem-solving skills.

Encouraging Positive Thinking and Growth Mindset

✔ **Embrace Challenges:**

Encouraging children to view challenges as opportunities for growth rather than threats is the first step in fostering a growth mindset. By embracing challenges, children learn to see setbacks as temporary and opportunities for learning and improvement. Parents can help cultivate this mindset by sharing stories of their challenges and how they overcame them. Through these narratives, children gain insight into the resilience and determination needed to overcome obstacles, inspiring them to approach challenges with a positive attitude and a willingness to persevere.

✔ **Praise Effort, Not Just Results:**

In a results-driven society, it's easy for children to equate success with achievement and outcomes. However, focusing solely on results can undermine the importance of effort and persistence in the learning process. Parents can shift this mindset by praising their children's effort and hard work, regardless of the outcome. By acknowledging the value of effort, children learn that success is not solely determined by innate ability but by the dedication and perseverance they invest in their pursuits. This reinforces the idea that improvement and growth come through continuous effort and learning, laying the foundation for a growth mindset.

✔ Reframe Negative Thoughts:

Negative thinking patterns, such as self-doubt and pessimism, can hinder children's ability to face challenges with confidence and resilience. Teaching children to recognize and challenge negative thoughts is essential for nurturing a positive mindset. Parents can encourage their children to reframe negative thoughts by replacing them with positive affirmations and constructive thinking. For example, instead of saying "I can't do this," children can learn to say "I can learn how to do this." By reframing negative thoughts, children develop a more optimistic outlook on challenges, empowering them to approach difficult situations with confidence and determination.

✔ Model Positive Thinking:

Parents serve as powerful role models for their children's attitudes and behaviors. By modeling positive thinking and resilience, parents can instill these qualities in their children. Sharing personal experiences of overcoming obstacles and maintaining a positive outlook demonstrates to children the power of positivity and resilience in the face of adversity. Positive coping mechanisms, like self-care, mindfulness, and gratitude practices, can also be modeled by parents for their kids to help them learn how to face difficulties head-on and with grace. Parents create the foundation for their children to develop a resilient attitude that will benefit them throughout their lives by demonstrating positive thinking consistently.

Promoting Healthy Coping Mechanisms

In the face of life's inevitable challenges and setbacks, the ability to cope effectively is essential for maintaining emotional well-being and resilience. As a parent, I've witnessed firsthand the transformative power of healthy coping mechanisms in my own child's life. When my son, James, faced difficulties with anxiety and stress, I realized the importance of equipping him with effective coping skills. Together, we embarked on a journey to explore various coping strategies, drawing on both professional guidance and personal insights. Through this process, I witnessed James develop resilience and emotional intelligence, empowering him to navigate life's challenges with confidence and grace.

I introduce him to stress management techniques that promote relaxation and emotional regulation, such as deep breathing exercises, mindfulness meditation, or progressive muscle relaxation. These techniques provide invaluable tools for managing stress and anxiety, enabling him to navigate challenging situations with calmness and clarity.

As a parent, you serve as a powerful role model for your child's coping behaviors. Demonstrating healthy coping strategies in your own life by managing stress effectively and seeking support when needed, sharing your experiences of overcoming challenges and the coping mechanisms you utilized help inspire your child to cultivate similar skills in their own life.

Over time, these strategies employed in promoting healthy coping mechanisms have had a profound and lasting impact on James's life. He has developed a repertoire of effective coping skills that enable him to manage stress, navigate challenges, and maintain emotional well-being. From utilizing mindfulness techniques to seeking support from trusted adults, James demonstrates resilience and maturity beyond his years. As a parent, witnessing his growth and development has reinforced the importance of nurturing healthy coping mechanisms in children, influencing my decision to share these insights in this book.

<u>*Positive Affirmations*</u> <u>for Building Resilience and Confidence</u>

<u>for Your Kid</u>

I am adaptable and can adjust to changes with ease.

I create structure and routine in my life to feel secure and confident.

I communicate openly and honestly with my family, building strong connections.

I am a problem-solver, finding solutions to challenges with creativity and resilience.

I express my emotions freely and manage them in healthy ways.

I create a safe and welcoming environment in my home where I can be myself.

I listen to others with empathy and understanding, building meaningful relationships.

I learn from my experiences and use them to grow and improve.

I am capable of handling whatever comes my way with grace and determination.

I respect myself and others, treating everyone with kindness and compassion.

I embrace new opportunities and challenges as chances to learn and grow.

I am mindful of my thoughts and actions, choosing positivity and optimism.

I take care of my physical, mental, and emotional well-being every day.

I am resilient and bounce back from difficulties stronger than before.

I am a valuable member of my family, contributing to our collective happiness and success.

Chapter Three

Navigating Challenges

Parenting is filled with many challenges that require patience, flexibility, and a willingness to adapt. One common difficulty is balancing the need to guide children with the necessity to let them express themselves. For example, Emilia, a mother who struggled with her son Carter's insistence on wearing dinosaur pajamas everywhere, initially felt frustrated and embarrassed. However, observing another parent allow their child to wear a Spider-Man costume year-round helped Emilia realize that embracing her son's unique preferences could make daily life more pleasant and harmonious.

Another major challenge is the conflicting advice parents often receive. Another mother, Catherine was overwhelmed by parenting books offering contradictory strategies. Trying to follow all this advice simultaneously led to confusion and frustration for her and her son. Through trial and error, Catherine learned that effective parenting often means adapting to the specific needs of the moment rather than rigidly adhering to any one method. This realization helped her focus on understanding and connecting with her child, rather than stressing over inconsistent techniques.

Balancing work and family life is another significant challenge. Many parents struggle to find enough time to spend with their children due to demanding work schedules. This can lead to feelings of guilt and stress, as they strive to meet their professional obligations while also being present for their children. Finding ways to prioritize family time, such as setting aside regular periods for activities and ensuring quality interactions, can help alleviate some of this pressure.

Managing behavioral issues is also a common parenting challenge. Children's tantrums, disagreements, and other behaviors can be exhausting to handle. Parents need to approach these situations with patience and understanding, recognizing that children are still learning how to manage their emotions and behaviors. Consistency and empathy are key in helping children develop appropriate ways to express themselves and interact with others.

Navigating social pressures is another hurdle. Parents often feel compelled to conform to societal expectations regarding parenting styles, educational choices, and even their children's appearances. These pressures can create anxiety and lead parents to make decisions based on external opinions rather than what is best for their family. Trusting their instincts and prioritizing their children's happiness and well-being over societal norms can help parents navigate these pressures more effectively.

The digital age brings unique challenges as well. Parents must monitor their children's screen time, understand the social platforms they use, and ensure their online safety. This requires staying informed about technological changes and teaching children about responsible digital behavior. Open communication about the benefits and risks of technology is crucial in helping children navigate the digital world safely.

Dealing with health issues, whether physical or mental, adds another layer of responsibility. Parents must ensure their children receive proper medical care, manage any chronic conditions, and support their overall well-being. This can be particularly stressful, but seeking appropriate medical advice and building a support network can make these challenges more manageable.

Ultimately, parenting is about embracing imperfection and focusing on the connection and happiness within the family. Accepting children as they are, with all their quirks and preferences, allows parents to enjoy the journey and turn everyday challenges into opportunities for growth and bonding. By letting go of the desire for perfection and instead prioritizing love, understanding, and acceptance, parents can create a more fulfilling and joyful parenting experience.

Addressing peer pressure and bullying in parenting requires a multifaceted approach that leverages emotional intelligence and supportive parenting styles. Recognizing the significant role of both interpersonal and intrapersonal intelligence, parents can create a nurturing environment that diminishes the likelihood of their children engaging in or falling victim to bullying. High-demanding and responsive parenting, which combines setting clear expectations with warmth and support, has been shown to significantly enhance emotional intelligence and reduce bullying behaviors.

As parents, we can help their children develop interpersonal intelligence by teaching them to recognize and understand others' emotions. This can be done through activities that encourage empathy, such as discussing feelings and role-playing different social scenarios. When children can empathize with others, they are less likely to engage in bullying and more likely to support peers who might be targeted. Furthermore, fostering intrapersonal intelligence is equally crucial. This involves helping children understand their own emotions, strengths, and weaknesses. Encouraging self-reflection and emotional regulation can lead to better self-control and resilience, reducing the likelihood of both bullying and being bullied.

The influence of peer pressure is another critical aspect parents must address. Peer pressure can drive children to conform to group norms, sometimes leading to aggressive behaviors like bullying. Encourage your child to make independent choices and reinforce the idea that it's okay to be different from their peers. This can be achieved by celebrating individuality and teaching them the importance of standing up for what is right, even if it means standing alone. Providing them with tools to assert themselves, such as effective communication skills and strategies to resist negative peer influence, can empower them to make positive decisions.

When children observe positive conflict resolution at home, they are more likely to emulate these behaviors in their interactions with peers. Moreover, parents should stay engaged with their children's social lives without being intrusive. This involves being aware of their friendships and the dynamics within their peer groups. Encouraging them to form friendships with peers who exhibit positive behaviors and values can create a supportive social network that buffers against bullying and peer pressure. Organizing group activities that promote teamwork and mutual respect can further reinforce these positive relationships.

In today's digital age, monitoring online interactions is essential. Cyberbullying is a pervasive issue that can have severe psychological impacts. Educate your child about the importance of digital citizenship and the potential consequences of their online actions. Setting clear guidelines for internet use and discussing the importance of privacy and respectful online behavior can help prevent cyberbullying.

Notably, collaborating with schools is vital. Schools play a significant role in shaping social interactions and addressing bullying. Maintaining open lines of communication with teachers and school administrators to stay informed about your child's social environment and any incidents of bullying is another important factor as Parents. Participating in school activities and supporting anti-bullying programs can strengthen these efforts and create a united front against bullying.

Parenting Through Transitions: Divorce, Relocation, Loss

As a parent who has deeply invested in the well-being of families, I understand the profound impact that transitions like divorce, relocation, and loss can have on children. Parenting through these difficult times requires patience, empathy, and resilience.

In the face of divorce, children may experience a whirlwind of emotions ranging from sadness and confusion to anger and fear. Parents must create a safe and supportive environment where children feel heard and valued. Open communication, honesty, and reassurance are key. By validating their feelings and providing consistent love and stability, parents can help children navigate the challenges of divorce with resilience.

Relocation can also pose unique challenges for families as children adjust to new environments, schools, and social circles. Parents can ease this transition by involving children in the decision-making process when possible and providing ample opportunities for exploration and connection in their new surroundings. Building a sense of belonging and security is essential during times of relocation, and parents can foster this by maintaining familiar routines, seeking out supportive community resources, and encouraging open dialogue about any concerns or fears.

Loss, whether it's the death of a loved one, a pet, or a significant change in circumstances, can be incredibly difficult for children to process. Parents play a critical role in helping children navigate grief and loss by offering comfort, empathy, and support. Encouraging children to express their emotions, memories, and questions can facilitate healing and understanding. Creating rituals or traditions to honor the memory of what's been lost can also provide comfort and closure for children as they grieve.

Throughout all these transitions, it's important for parents to prioritize self-care and seek support for themselves as well. Together, families can navigate transitions with compassion, resilience, and strength, emerging stronger and more connected on the other side.

Daily ACTIONS

Daily Check-Ins: Regularly ask your child about their day, paying attention to any signs of distress or unusual behavior. Create a habit of open communication where they feel comfortable sharing their experiences with you.

Role-Play Scenarios: Engage in role-playing exercises with your child to help them practice assertive responses to peer pressure situations. Use real-life scenarios to simulate various social interactions and empower them to make confident choices.

Positive Affirmations: Provide daily affirmations and encouragement to boost your child's self-esteem and resilience. Remind them of their strengths and capabilities, reinforcing their sense of self-worth.

Teach Problem-Solving Skills: Encourage your child to brainstorm solutions to social challenges they may encounter, fostering their problem-solving abilities. Guide them in considering different perspectives and evaluating potential outcomes.

Model Empathy and Kindness: Demonstrate empathy and kindness in your interactions with others, serving as a positive role model for your child. Encourage acts of kindness towards peers and emphasize the importance of treating others with respect.

Discuss Peer Dynamics: Initiate conversations about peer dynamics and the influence of group behavior on individual choices. Help your child understand the concept of peer pressure and brainstorm strategies for navigating social situations with integrity.

Monitor Online Activity: Regularly monitor your child's online activity and engage in discussions about responsible internet use. Set boundaries around screen time and establish guidelines for safe and respectful online behavior.

Encourage Diverse Friendships: Encourage your child to cultivate friendships with peers from diverse backgrounds and interests. Emphasize the value of building relationships based on mutual respect and shared values rather than conformity to peer norms.

Promote Teamwork and Collaboration: Facilitate opportunities for your child to participate in group activities and collaborative projects. Encourage teamwork, communication, and mutual support within these contexts, fostering positive social skills.

Seek Support When Needed: Be proactive in seeking support from teachers, counselors, or mental health professionals if you notice persistent issues related to peer pressure or bullying. Collaborate with school staff and community resources to address concerns and provide additional support for your child's well-being.

<u>*Positive Affirmations*</u> for Building Resilience and Confidence for Your Kid

"I embrace my uniqueness and express myself authentically."

"I adapt to changes with resilience and grace."

"I trust my instincts and make decisions that are right for me."

"I am patient with myself and others as we navigate challenges together."

"I am open to learning and growing from every experience."

"I communicate my feelings and concerns openly and honestly."

"I surround myself with supportive friends and family who uplift me."

"I am capable of handling difficult situations with courage and determination."

"I set boundaries that honor my well-being and respect others."

"I find strength in adversity and emerge stronger than before."

"I choose kindness and empathy in all my interactions."

"I let go of perfectionism and embrace the beauty of imperfection."

"I focus on solutions rather than dwelling on problems."

"I celebrate my achievements, no matter how small they may seem."

"I am resilient, and I believe in my ability to overcome any obstacle."

Chapter Four

Parenting Approaches for Different Types of Children

Understanding Stubborn Kids

Stubborn kids are those who really stick to their own ideas and sometimes don't like to listen to others, like parents or teachers. I remember one time when my daughter, Emily, who is quite stubborn, refused to wear anything other than her favorite purple dress to school, even though it was dirty. Instead of getting frustrated, I realized that she just wanted to feel like she had some say in what she wore. So, I gave her two choices: either she could wear the purple dress or she could choose another outfit that she liked. This way, she felt like she had some control over the situation, and she ended up picking a different dress herself.

It's important to understand that stubborn kids aren't trying to be difficult on purpose. They just want to feel like they have some independence and that their opinions matter. So, as parents, we can help by giving them options and letting them make decisions when it's appropriate. We also need to be firm about important rules and consequences, but still show them love and support. With Emily, I've found that when I acknowledge her feelings and give her a little space to make her own choices, she's more willing to cooperate and listen.

Stubborn kids, like Emily, often have a strong will and a firm belief in their own ideas. They can be quite determined and persistent, which are actually valuable traits when channeled positively. For instance, Emily's stubbornness has helped her excel in her art projects. Once she sets her mind on creating something, she puts in the time and effort to make it happen, even if it means facing challenges along the way.

As parents, it's important for us to recognize and respect our child's autonomy while also guiding them toward making responsible choices. For example, when Emily was adamant about wanting to stay up late to finish a drawing, I explained the importance of getting enough rest for her health and school performance. Instead of simply saying "no," I offered her the choice of either finishing her drawing the next day or managing her time more efficiently so she could complete it earlier. This approach allowed her to feel empowered while also learning about prioritization and self-discipline.

Moreover, stubborn kids often respond well to positive reinforcement and encouragement. When Emily puts in effort to complete a challenging task, I make sure to praise her perseverance and determination. By celebrating her achievements, big or small, I reinforce the idea that hard work and persistence pay off.

Nurturing World-Changing Kids

World-changing kids possess a natural inclination towards empathy, compassion, and a desire to make a difference in the world around them. As parents, nurturing these qualities involves fostering their innate sense of altruism and social responsibility. Nurturing world-changing kids involves recognizing their innate empathy, compassion, and desire to make a difference in the world. These children naturally gravitate towards acts of kindness and are deeply concerned about global issues. As parents, our role is to support and encourage these qualities, helping our children realize their potential to impact the world positively.

One way to nurture world-changing kids is by involving them in community service activities. Participating in volunteer work, such as helping at a local shelter or participating in environmental clean-up efforts, allows children to understand the importance of giving back to their community and caring for others. These experiences also teach valuable lessons about empathy, cooperation, and the power of collective action.

It's also essential to expose children to diverse perspectives and global issues. Engaging in open discussions about topics like poverty, inequality, and environmental sustainability helps broaden their understanding of the world and encourages them to think critically about how they can contribute to positive change. Watching educational documentaries, reading books, and exploring different cultures further enrich their knowledge and perspective.

As parents, we play a crucial role in modeling empathy and compassion in our everyday actions. By treating others with kindness and respect, whether it's helping a neighbor in need or advocating for social justice causes, we demonstrate the values we hope to instill in our children. Through our actions, children learn that compassion isn't just a concept – it's a fundamental aspect of how we interact with the world around us.

Supporting Intellectual Kids

Intellectual kids demonstrate a keen curiosity and a voracious appetite for learning. Supporting these children involves creating an environment that nurtures their intellectual development and encourages their thirst for knowledge. Providing access to stimulating educational resources, such as books, puzzles, and educational games, can help satisfy their intellectual curiosity and promote continuous learning. Offering opportunities for hands-on exploration and experimentation allows them to delve deeper into subjects of interest and develop critical thinking skills. Additionally, fostering a love of learning involves celebrating their achievements and encouraging a growth mindset, emphasizing the value of effort and perseverance over innate ability. Creating a supportive and stimulating home environment where intellectual pursuits are encouraged can help intellectual kids thrive and reach their full potential.

Supporting intellectual kids involves recognizing and nurturing their innate curiosity and hunger for knowledge. These children possess a natural inclination towards exploring and understanding the world around them, often displaying a remarkable capacity for absorbing information and making connections.

One way to support intellectual kids is by providing them with access to a wide range of stimulating educational resources. Books, puzzles, educational games, and interactive learning tools can help satisfy their curiosity and fuel their passion for learning. These materials offer avenues for exploration and discovery, allowing children to delve deeper into subjects that captivate their interest. Encouraging hands-on exploration and experimentation is another crucial aspect of supporting intellectual kids. Providing opportunities for them to engage in activities like science experiments, art projects, or building projects fosters their creativity and critical thinking skills. These experiences not only stimulate their intellectual growth but also encourage them to develop problem-solving abilities and innovative thinking.

Also, celebrating their achievements and fostering a growth mindset is essential for intellectual kids. Instead of focusing solely on outcomes, parents can praise their efforts and perseverance, emphasizing the value of learning and personal growth. By instilling a belief in their ability to overcome challenges and learn from mistakes, parents can help intellectual kids develop resilience and a lifelong love of learning. Meanwhile, creating a supportive and stimulating home environment is key to helping intellectual kids thrive. This involves fostering an atmosphere where curiosity is encouraged, questions are welcomed, and intellectual pursuits are celebrated. By nurturing their passion for learning and providing opportunities for exploration and discovery, parents can empower intellectual kids to reach their full potential and pursue their academic interests with confidence.

Other Categories of children and some tailored parenting approaches

1. The Sensitive Child:

- Characteristics: These children are highly attuned to their emotions and the emotions of others. They may be more prone to anxiety or overwhelmed in certain situations.

- Parenting Approach: Offer plenty of reassurance and emotional support. Create a calm and nurturing environment at home. Teach them coping strategies for managing strong emotions, such as deep breathing or mindfulness exercises. Validate their feelings and help them develop resilience.

2. The Spirited Child:

- Characteristics: Spirited children are energetic, enthusiastic, and often have strong opinions. They may be more intense in their reactions and behaviors.

✔ Parenting Approach: Provide outlets for their energy and creativity, such as sports or artistic activities. Set clear boundaries and expectations, but allow for flexibility and negotiation when appropriate. Offer positive reinforcement for their efforts and achievements. Help them channel their enthusiasm into constructive outlets.

3. The Shy or Introverted Child:

- Characteristics: These children may be more reserved in social situations and take longer to warm up to new people or environments. They may prefer solitary activities over group settings.

✔ Parenting Approach: Respect their need for space and quiet time. Encourage social interactions at their own pace, but don't force them into situations that make them uncomfortable. Provide opportunities for them to build social skills gradually, such as one-on-one playdates or small group activities. Offer praise and encouragement for their efforts to step outside their comfort zone.

4. The Strong-Willed Child:

- Characteristics: Strong-willed children are independent, determined, and often assertive. They may challenge rules and authority figures and resist being told what to do.

✔ Parenting Approach: Set clear and consistent boundaries, but

be prepared to negotiate and compromise when necessary. Offer choices whenever possible to give them a sense of autonomy and control. Provide opportunities for them to use their leadership skills in positive ways, such as organizing activities or projects. Stay calm and patient during power struggles, and focus on problem-solving rather than punishment.

5. The Highly Sensitive Child:

- Characteristics: Highly sensitive children are deeply affected by their environment and may be more reactive to sensory stimuli such as noise, light, or texture. They may also be more empathetic and compassionate towards others.

✔ Parenting Approach: Create a calm and predictable

environment to help minimize sensory overload. Be mindful of their sensitivities and avoid overwhelming them with too much stimulation. Teach them self-care strategies for managing overwhelm, such as taking breaks in quiet spaces or using sensory tools like fidget toys. Encourage them to embrace their empathy and compassion, and teach them how to set healthy boundaries to protect their own emotional well-being.

6. The Attention-Seeking Child:

- Characteristics: These children crave attention and may resort to negative behaviors to get it. They may be disruptive or act out in order to gain recognition.

- ✔ Parenting Approach: Provide positive attention and praise for

  desirable behaviors, rather than focusing solely on negative behaviors. Set aside dedicated one-on-one time with them each day to give them the attention they crave in a positive way. Teach them alternative ways to seek attention, such as asking for help or sharing their accomplishments with others. Encourage them to develop hobbies or interests where they can shine and receive positive feedback.

7. The Perfectionist Child:

- Characteristics: Perfectionist children have high standards for themselves and may become overly critical or anxious if they don't meet those standards. They may avoid trying new things or taking risks for fear of failure.

✔ Parenting Approach: Foster a growth mindset by emphasizing effort and progress over perfection. Encourage them to take risks and try new things, even if they might fail. Teach them that mistakes are a natural part of learning and growth. Offer praise and validation for their efforts, regardless of the outcome. Help them develop healthy coping strategies for managing stress and anxiety, such as deep breathing or positive self-talk.

8. The Resenting Child:

- Resenting children harbor feelings of anger, bitterness, or resentment, often towards their parents or other authority figures. They may perceive themselves as victims of unfair treatment or neglect, leading to defiance and hostility. Parenting these children requires addressing underlying issues and rebuilding trust and rapport. Listening to their concerns without judgment, acknowledging their feelings, and offering reassurance can help mend the parent-child relationship. Implementing consistent discipline with clear boundaries, coupled with empathy and understanding, can gradually alleviate resentment and foster a more positive dynamic within the family. Additionally, providing opportunities for open communication and family therapy may be beneficial in addressing deep-seated issues and facilitating healing.

<u>*Positive Affirmations*</u> <u>for Building Resilience and Confidence for Your Kid</u>

"I am capable of finding creative solutions to any problem I encounter."

"I embrace change as an opportunity for growth and discovery."

"I trust myself to make choices that align with my values and beliefs."

"I welcome challenges as stepping stones toward achieving my goals."

"I am worthy of love and acceptance just as I am."

"I forgive myself for mistakes and use them as lessons for improvement."

"I deserve to take breaks and care for my mental and physical well-being."

"I am surrounded by people who believe in me and support my dreams."

"I am a valuable member of my community, and my contributions matter."

"I am patient with myself as I learn and grow each day."

"I trust that setbacks are temporary and opportunities for learning."

"I am curious and embrace new experiences with enthusiasm."

"I am resilient, and I bounce back stronger from life's challenges."

"I listen to my intuition and make decisions that feel right for me."

"I am grateful for the abundance of blessings and opportunities in my life."

Chapter Five

Self-Care for Parents

Taking care of yourself as a parent is super important but sometimes gets forgotten. When you're busy looking after your kids, it's easy to forget about your own needs. But looking after yourself is really important for your body and mind. It helps you feel better, and when you feel better, you can be a better parent to your kids.

First off, taking care of yourself means looking after your body. That means eating healthy food, doing some exercise, and making sure you get enough sleep. When you do these things, you have more energy to keep up with your kids and do all the things you need to do every day. Then there's your mind and feelings. Being a parent can be stressful sometimes, and it's okay to feel a bit overwhelmed. But it's important to take care of your mental health too. That might mean doing things like taking a few minutes to relax, writing down your thoughts in a journal, or talking to someone if you're feeling really stressed out.

Furthermore, self-care encompasses strategies to safeguard and nurture one's mental and emotional well-being. The daily challenges and stressors of parenting can take a toll on parents' mental health, leading to feelings of overwhelm, anxiety, and even depression.

Neglecting one's mental and emotional needs not only undermines parental well-being but can also impact the quality of the parent-child relationship. By prioritizing self-care, parents can cultivate resilience and emotional balance, enabling them to respond to challenges with equanimity and grace. This may involve practices such as mindfulness meditation, journaling, or seeking therapy or counseling to process and manage difficult emotions effectively.

And here's the cool part: when you take care of yourself, it's not just good for you—it's good for your kids too! Kids can tell when their parents are happy and relaxed, and it makes them feel happy too. So, by looking after yourself, you're also looking after your kids. In the end, taking care of yourself isn't selfish—it's actually really important for being the best parent you can be. When you take care of yourself, you have more energy, you feel better, and you can be there for your kids in the best way possible. Now let's look at the importance of self-care as parents.

Importance of Self-Care in Parenting

Taking care of yourself as a parent is really, really important. It's like when you're on an airplane, and they tell you to put on your own oxygen mask before helping others. That's because if you don't take care of yourself first, it's hard to take care of anyone else properly. When parents forget about their own needs and just focus on their kids, they can start feeling really stressed, tired, and just not themselves. And when parents feel like that, it's tough for them to be the loving, patient, and supportive parents their kids need. But when parents make self-care a priority, it's like giving themselves a little boost of energy and happiness. They can recharge their batteries, feel less stressed, and just feel better overall. And when parents feel good, they can be there for their kids in the best possible way—listening, playing, and helping them out when they need it.

So, taking care of yourself isn't just something nice to do—it's really important for being the best parent you can be. It's like filling up your tank so you have plenty of gas to keep going, and to be there for your kids every step of the way.

Imagine a bustling household where parents are juggling work, chores, and the demands of daily life. In the midst of this whirlwind, it's easy for parents to feel stressed, tired, and overwhelmed. But what many parents don't realize is that this stress can have a profound impact on their relationship with their children. When parents are constantly stressed or exhausted, it can show in their interactions with their kids. They might find themselves snapping over minor issues or lacking the patience to listen when their children want to talk. This can leave kids feeling confused, sad, or like they're not important enough to warrant their parents' attention.

However, when parents prioritize self-care, it can completely transform the family dynamic. By taking time to look after their own physical, mental, and emotional well-being, parents are better equipped to handle the ups and downs of parenthood with grace and patience. This creates a warm and nurturing environment at home where kids feel valued, supported, and loved.

Moreover, practicing self-care sets a powerful example for children, teaching them the importance of prioritizing their own well-being. When kids see their parents making time for activities that bring them joy and relaxation, they learn that self-care is an essential part of a balanced and fulfilling life. But the benefits of self-care extend far beyond just the parent-child relationship. When parents feel good physically, mentally, and emotionally, they have more energy and enthusiasm to engage with their children in meaningful ways. Whether it's playing games, reading stories, or embarking on adventures together, these shared experiences strengthen the bond between parent and child and create lasting memories.

Some of the importance of self-care is summarized below;

- **Enhanced Well-being:** Self-care practices like exercise, adequate sleep, and relaxation techniques contribute to better physical, mental, and emotional health for parents.

- **Reduced Stress:** Taking time for self-care helps parents manage stress levels more effectively, reducing the risk of burnout and emotional exhaustion.

- **Improved Parent-Child Relationships:** When parents prioritize self-care, they can be more patient, attentive, and emotionally available for their children, fostering stronger and healthier relationships.

- **Positive Role Modeling:** Demonstrating self-care teaches children the importance of looking after their own well-being and sets a positive example for healthy living habits.

- **Increased Energy and Engagement:** Self-care practices replenish parents' energy reserves, allowing them to engage more actively in family activities and create positive experiences with their children.

- **Enhanced Resilience:** Engaging in self-care activities builds resilience, helping parents cope better with the challenges and demands of parenting.

- **Better Decision Making:** Taking regular breaks and practicing self-care improves cognitive function and decision-making abilities, enabling parents to make sound choices for their families.

☐ **Emotional Regulation:** Self-care strategies like mindfulness and relaxation techniques equip parents with the tools to manage their emotions more effectively, promoting a calm and supportive parenting environment.

☐ **Overall Family Well-being:** Prioritizing self-care contributes to a happier, healthier family dynamic, fostering an environment where everyone feels valued, supported, and nurtured.

Managing Parental Stress and Burnout

Managing parental stress and burnout is a significant component of self-care. Parenting can be challenging and demanding, and it's natural for parents to experience stress and feelings of overwhelm from time to time. However, chronic stress and burnout can have detrimental effects on both physical and mental health, leading to fatigue, irritability, and feelings of inadequacy. To prevent burnout, parents must learn to recognize the signs of stress and prioritize activities that promote relaxation, rejuvenation, and emotional balance. This may involve practicing mindfulness or meditation, engaging in regular exercise, seeking support from friends or family members, or pursuing hobbies and interests that bring joy and fulfillment.

Things TO DO

✔ **Take breaks:** Schedule regular breaks throughout the day to relax and recharge, even if it's just for a few minutes at a time.

✔ **Practice deep breathing:** Incorporate deep breathing exercises into your daily routine to help calm your mind and reduce stress.

✔ **Prioritize sleep:** Aim for a consistent sleep schedule and ensure you're getting enough rest each night to feel refreshed and rejuvenated.

✔ **Engage in physical activity:** Incorporate regular exercise into your routine, whether it's going for a walk, practicing yoga, or participating in a fitness class.

✔ **Seek social support:** Reach out to friends, family members, or support groups for encouragement and understanding during challenging times.

✔ **Set realistic expectations:** Be realistic about what you can accomplish in a day and avoid putting too much pressure on yourself to be perfect.

✔ **Delegate tasks:** Delegate household chores and responsibilities to other family members to lighten your load and create more time for self-care.

✔ **Practice mindfulness:** Incorporate mindfulness techniques, such as meditation or journaling, to help you stay present and manage stress more effectively.

✔ **Engage in enjoyable activities:** Make time for hobbies and activities that bring you joy and relaxation, whether it's reading, gardening, or listening to music.

✔ **Seek professional help:** Don't hesitate to seek support from a therapist or counselor if you're struggling to cope with stress and burnout on your own.

Setting Boundaries and Prioritizing Self-Care

Setting boundaries and prioritizing self-care are essential strategies for maintaining balance and well-being as a parent. It's important for parents to establish clear boundaries around their time, energy, and resources, and to communicate their needs effectively with their family members. This may involve saying no to additional commitments or responsibilities, delegating tasks to others, or seeking outside help when needed. By setting boundaries and prioritizing self-care, parents can create space for rest, relaxation, and rejuvenation, allowing them to show up as their best selves for their children.

✔ **Schedule regular "me time":** Set aside dedicated time each day or week for self-care activities that rejuvenate you, whether it's taking a bath, reading a book, or going for a walk.

✔ **Communicate your needs:** Communicate your needs and boundaries to your family members, ensuring they understand when you need time alone or assistance with household tasks.

✔ **Say no when necessary:** Learn to say no to additional commitments or requests that may overwhelm you or interfere with your self-care routine.

✔ **Establish technology boundaries:** Set boundaries around your use of technology, such as limiting screen time and creating tech-free zones in the home to promote relaxation and connection.

✔ **Practice self-compassion:** Be kind to yourself and recognize that it's okay to prioritize your well-being and set boundaries to protect your mental and emotional health.

✔ **Create a self-care plan:** Develop a personalized self-care plan that outlines specific activities and practices you can incorporate into your routine to promote overall well-being.

✔ **Reflect and adjust:** Regularly reflect on your self-care practices and boundaries, and make adjustments as needed to ensure they continue to meet your evolving needs as a parent

Positive Affirmations for Parental Guidance and Love

"I am a beacon of love, guiding my child through life's journey with unwavering compassion."

"Every moment with my child is a precious gift, and I cherish each one with boundless gratitude."

"I am a nurturing force, fostering growth, and resilience in my child with every embrace."

"In the dance of parenthood, I lead with grace and confidence, knowing that each step is a beautiful part of our shared journey."

"I am a constant source of strength and support for my child, lifting them up with words of encouragement and acts of kindness."

"My love for my child knows no bounds, flowing endlessly like a river of light and warmth."

"I am a guiding light in my child's life, illuminating their path with wisdom, compassion, and unwavering belief."

"With every hug, I envelop my child in a cocoon of safety and security, letting them know they are always protected."

"I am a steadfast anchor in the stormy seas of life, providing stability and reassurance to my child through every challenge."

"My words are like seeds of affirmation, planting the roots of confidence and self-love deep within my child's heart."

"I am a master builder, shaping the foundation of my child's future with love, patience, and unwavering dedication."

"In the garden of parenthood, I cultivate a rich soil of empathy and understanding, nurturing my child's growth with tender care."

"My presence is a source of comfort and joy for my child, wrapping them in a warm embrace of unconditional love."

"I am a guardian of dreams, encouraging my child to reach for the stars and never lose sight of their limitless potential."

"With every smile, I paint a rainbow of happiness across my child's sky, filling their world with vibrant colors and endless possibilities."

"I am a warrior of love, fearlessly protecting my child's innocence and purity from the harshness of the world."

"My voice is a melody of encouragement, lifting my child's spirits and inspiring them to soar to new heights."

"I am a lighthouse of guidance, shining brightly through the darkness to lead my child safely home."

"With every heartbeat, I send waves of love and strength to my child, enveloping them in a blanket of warmth and security."

"I am a guardian angel, watching over my child with unwavering devotion and boundless love."

"My arms are a sanctuary of comfort, offering solace and protection to my child whenever they need it."

"I am a storyteller of dreams, weaving tales of hope and inspiration that ignite the imagination of my child."

"In the tapestry of life, I am the thread that binds my family together with love, unity, and unwavering support."

"I am a mirror of reflection, showing my child the beauty and brilliance that lies within them."

"My love is a guiding compass, pointing my child towards their true north with unwavering clarity and purpose."

"I am a conductor of joy, orchestrating moments of laughter and happiness that fill my child's heart with pure delight."

"With every step, I walk beside my child, offering guidance, encouragement, and unwavering belief in their abilities."

"I am a fountain of wisdom, sharing the lessons of life with my child and guiding them towards a future filled with promise."

"My embrace is a sanctuary of peace, enveloping my child in a blanket of serenity and calm."

"I am a guardian of dreams, nurturing the seeds of imagination and creativity that bloom within my child's soul."

"With every word, I plant seeds of positivity and affirmation in my child's mind, cultivating a garden of confidence and self-love."

"I am a beacon of hope, lighting the way forward for my child with unwavering faith and optimism."

"My love is a shield of protection, guarding my child from harm and surrounding them with a fortress of safety."

"I am a symphony of love, harmonizing with my child's heartbeats to create a melody of joy and happiness."

"With every embrace, I wrap my child in a blanket of love, filling their world with warmth and tenderness."

"I am a guardian of innocence, preserving the magic and wonder of childhood for my child to cherish forever."

"My words are like seeds of wisdom, planting the roots of knowledge and understanding deep within my child's soul."

"I am a bridge of connection, spanning the gap between generations with love, respect, and understanding."

"With every kiss, I shower my child with blessings, infusing their spirit with love, joy, and endless possibilities."

"I am a beacon of strength, standing tall and proud for my child, inspiring them to face life's challenges with courage and resilience."

Chapter Six

Guiding Your Child to Choose the Right Career Path

A Parent's Role in Encouraging Free Will

Did you know that 70% of students/children, and teenagers, feel pressured by their parents when choosing a career path?

Understanding the importance of free will

When it comes to choosing a career, allowing children to exercise their own free will is crucial. This might seem daunting to a parent, but it's essential for their long-term happiness and success. When children feel they have control over their career choices, they are more likely to be motivated and committed to their work. This intrinsic motivation, driven by personal interest and passion, leads to higher job satisfaction and better performance.

Why does Free Will Matter?

Studies have shown that individuals who choose their careers based on their own interests and strengths tend to be more successful and fulfilled. When parents impose their own career choices on their children, it can lead to resentment, lack of motivation, and even career burnout. On the other hand, supporting your child's autonomy helps them develop critical decision-making skills and a stronger sense of self.

Benefits of Autonomy:

1. Enhanced Motivation: Children are more likely to put effort into something they are genuinely interested in. This natural enthusiasm translates into a greater willingness to overcome challenges and persist through difficulties.

2. Increased Satisfaction: Choosing a career that aligns with personal interests and values leads to a higher level of job satisfaction. When people love what they do, it doesn't feel like work, and they're more likely to excel and innovate in their field.

3. Better Mental Health: Allowing children to follow their own career paths can also have positive effects on their mental health. They are less likely to experience the stress and anxiety that comes from trying to meet external expectations and more likely to find joy and fulfillment in their professional lives.

Statistical Evidence

Research from the Journal of Vocational Behavior indicates that individuals who feel autonomous in their career decisions report higher levels of job satisfaction and overall well-being. Furthermore, a study by the American Psychological Association found that young adults who perceived higher levels of parental support for autonomy had better psychological health outcomes.

Anecdote

Let's take the example of Sarah, a high school student who loved art but whose parents insisted she pursue a career in medicine. Despite excelling academically, Sarah felt unfulfilled and stressed. When her parents finally supported her decision to study graphic design, she thrived, eventually landing a job at a top design firm and finding true happiness in her work. This story highlights how crucial it is to respect and support your child's own career choices.

Common Mistakes Parents Make

1. Imposing their own unfulfilled dreams

One common mistake parents make is imposing their own unfulfilled dreams on their children. It's natural to want your child to achieve what you couldn't, but this can place undue pressure on them and may lead to resentment and dissatisfaction.

Understanding the Impact

- **Loss of Identity:** When parents project their own dreams onto their children, it can overshadow the child's personal interests and aspirations. This can lead to a loss of identity, where the child feels they are living someone else's life.

- **Pressure and Stress:** Children may feel immense pressure to meet their parents' expectations, which can lead to stress, anxiety, and even burnout. This pressure can stifle their natural talents and creativity.

- **Resentment and Rebellion:** Imposing unfulfilled dreams can also create resentment. Children might comply initially but could eventually rebel, either by abandoning the chosen path or distancing themselves emotionally from their parents.

Anecdote

Lisa, whose father always dreamed of being a professional athlete but ended up in a different career. He pushed Lisa into sports from a young age, ignoring her interest in music. Despite her success in athletics, Lisa felt unfulfilled and resented her father's imposition. When she finally pursued her passion for music, she found joy and success, but the journey was fraught with emotional challenges.

2. Overemphasizing job security over passion

Another common mistake parents often make is prioritizing job security over their child's passion when it comes to career choices. While it's natural to want your child to have a stable and financially secure future, it's equally important to consider their interests and passions. Job security is important, but when it's the sole focus, it can overshadow a child's natural talents and interests. This can lead to a career that feels more like a burden than a fulfilling path. Passion is what drives creativity, innovation, and long-term satisfaction in one's career.

Why Passion Matters?

- **Intrinsic Motivation:** When people are passionate about their work, they are more likely to be intrinsically motivated. This means they are driven by internal rewards such as personal satisfaction and enjoyment rather than external rewards like salary or job security alone.
- **Long-Term Success:** Passion fuels persistence. In any career, there will be challenges and setbacks. Those who are passionate about their field are more likely to persevere through tough times because they are doing what they love.
- **Innovation and Creativity:** Passion often leads to higher levels of creativity and innovation. When individuals are genuinely interested in their work, they are more likely to think outside the box and come up with unique solutions and ideas.

Potential Downsides of Focusing Solely on Job Security:

- Lack of Engagement: A career chosen solely for job security can lead to disengagement and lack of enthusiasm. Over time, this can result in lower job performance and even burnout.
- Missed Opportunities for Fulfillment: By way of ignoring their passions, individuals may miss out on discovering their true potential and finding a career that they truly enjoy. This can lead to regret and a feeling of 'what if' later in life.

o   Mental Health Implications: Choosing a career that does not align with one's interests can also have negative implications for mental health, including increased stress, anxiety, and dissatisfaction.

Anecdote

Let's consider the story of Mark, who was pushed into a career in accounting because it promised stability and a good salary. Despite his success on paper, Mark felt unfulfilled and yearned for a more creative outlet. Eventually, he took the risk of pursuing his passion for photography and found not only personal satisfaction but also professional success as his work gained recognition. This shift improved his overall well-being and happiness.

3. Ignoring the child's interests and strengths

Another mistake is ignoring the child's interests and strengths. Each child is unique, with their own set of talents and passions. Overlooking these can result in a misaligned career path that doesn't leverage their full potential.

Understanding the Impact

- **Underutilized Potential:** When parents ignore their child's interests and strengths, they may push them towards careers that don't align with their natural abilities. This can result in underutilized potential and lack of engagement.
- **Lack of Motivation:** Children are more motivated and perform better when they are interested in what they are doing. Ignoring their interests can lead to disengagement and lackluster performance in both academics and professional life.
- **Decreased Self-Esteem:** When children are not encouraged to pursue what they are good at and passionate about, it can

affect their self-esteem. They might start to doubt their abilities and feel less confident in their career choices.

Steps to help your Child choose their Career Path

1. Encourage Exploration

Support Diverse Experiences: Allow your child to explore a variety of fields through internships, part-time jobs, volunteer work, and extracurricular activities. These experiences provide valuable insights into different professions and help your child discover what they enjoy and where their strengths lie. For instance, if your child shows an interest in healthcare, encourage them to volunteer at a hospital or shadow a healthcare professional.

Promote Hobbies and Interests: Support your child's hobbies and interests outside of academics. These activities can often lead to discovering potential career paths. If your child loves drawing, for instance, they might consider careers in graphic design, animation, or architecture.

2. Open Communication

Create a Safe Space for Dialogue: Maintain open and honest communication with your child about their career aspirations. Ask open-ended questions to understand their interests and listen actively without judgment. For instance, ask questions like, 'what subjects do you enjoy the most and why?', 'What kind of activities make you lose track of time?', 'What kind of work do you see yourself doing in the future?' or 'What activities make them feel fulfilled?'. Listen actively and without judgment, showing that you respect and value their opinions.

This approach helps your child feel valued and understood.

Regular Check-Ins: Have regular discussions about their goals and experiences. This ongoing dialogue helps you stay informed about their evolving interests and provides opportunities for you to offer guidance and support.

3. Provide Resources

Offer Tools, Not Decisions: Provide your child with resources such as career assessment tests, informational books, websites, and access to career counseling services. These tools can help them better understand their strengths, interests, and potential career paths. Introduce them to resources like the Myers-Briggs Type Indicator (MBTI) or the Strong Interest Inventory to help them identify careers that match their personality and interests.

Professional Counseling: Consider enlisting the help of a career counselor or coach base on your financial strength. These professionals can offer personalized advice and support, helping your child navigate their career options more effectively.

4. Support Decision-Making

Equip Them with Decision-Making Techniques: Help your child develop critical decision-making skills. Encourage them to research different careers, weigh the pros and cons, and consider long-term goals. Teach them to make informed decisions by evaluating various factors such as job responsibilities, work environment, salary, and growth opportunities.

Empower Them to Take Responsibility: Encourage your child to take ownership of their career decisions. This empowerment builds confidence and helps them develop the skills they need to navigate their career journey independently.

Guide them through a decision-making process for choosing courses or extracurricular activities, and discuss the potential impacts of each choice

5. Encourage Skill Development

Focus on Transferable Skills: Encourage your child to develop a broad set of skills that are valuable in any career, such as communication, problem-solving, teamwork, and time management. These transferable skills enhance their employability and adaptability in a rapidly changing job market.

Support Education and Training: Help your child identify educational and training opportunities that align with their career interests. This could include college degrees, vocational training, certifications, workshops, or online courses.

6. Focus on Strengths and Interests

Highlight Their Unique Qualities: Encourage your child to pursue careers that align with their natural talents and passions. Help them identify what they excel at and what they enjoy doing, and explore how these can translate into a fulfilling career.

If your child is good at math and enjoys problem-solving, suggest exploring careers in engineering, data science, or finance.

7. Support and Validate Their Choices

Be Their Cheerleader: Provide positive reinforcement and celebrate their efforts and achievements, no matter how small. Show your child that you trust their judgment and believe in their ability to make the right choices for themselves.

Understand that career paths are often non-linear and your child's interests may evolve over time. Be flexible and supportive of their changing aspirations, and encourage them to view career development as a lifelong journey.

Remind your child that it's okay to change directions and that many successful people have taken various paths before finding their ideal career

If your child decides to switch their major or career path, support their decision and discuss the new opportunities it presents.

8. Be a Role Model

Demonstrate a Positive Attitude towards Work: Show enthusiasm and a positive attitude toward your own career. Share your work experiences and the lessons you've learned. Your attitude towards work can influence your child's perspective on careers and job satisfaction.

Show Flexibility and Adaptability: Demonstrate the importance of being flexible and adaptable in your own career. Share stories about how you've navigated career changes or challenges. This helps your child understand that career paths are not always linear and that adaptability is a valuable trait.

Reducing Imposition

As parents, it's natural to want the best for our children, but imposing our own expectations and dreams on them can hinder their ability to find and pursue their true passions. To foster a supportive environment, it's important to reduce imposition and encourage their autonomy. Take time to reflect on why you have certain career expectations for your child. Are they based on your own unfulfilled dreams or societal pressures? Understanding your motivations can help you separate them from your child's interests. I recommend this four strategies to reduce the imposition

✔ Identify reasons behind career expectations for your child

✔ Recognize Bias: Be aware of your own biases and separate them from your child's interests.

✔ Respect Their Choices: Trust your child's judgment and support their decisions, even if they differ from your expectations.

✔ Positive Reinforcement: Provide positive feedback and encouragement throughout their exploration and decision-making process.

Conclusion

Throughout this book, we've explored many ways to become better parents. We've discussed how to help our kids feel strong and brave, handle tough situations, and prioritize self-care. Now that you're finishing this book, take a moment to reflect on what you've learned and how you can share positive messages with your child(ren). You've discovered that saying kind words to your child(ren) can boost their self-esteem, and listening to them and offering support when needed is crucial.

As a parent, you've come to understand that making mistakes is okay. Everyone makes mistakes, but what's important is learning from them. You've also realized the importance of taking care of yourself, as it allows you to better care for your child(ren). As you bid farewell to this book, remember the valuable lessons you've learned and continue applying them in your family life. Keep nurturing love, compassion, and strength as a parent, and always remember that when your family sticks together, there's nothing you can't overcome.

BONUS

Day 1:

Understand Your Parenting Style

- Reflect on your current parenting style.
- Identify strengths and areas for improvement.
- Set goals for the next 30 days.

Day 2:

Establish Clear Communication

- Practice active listening with your child.
- Encourage open and honest dialogue.
- Set a daily time for family conversations.

Day 3:

Create a Positive Environment

- Decorate a space for your child that promotes positivity.
- Display affirmations and motivational quotes.
- Celebrate small achievements together.

Day 4:

Set Consistent Routines

- Develop a daily schedule that includes family time, study time, and playtime.
- Stick to regular meal and bedtime routines.
- Discuss the importance of consistency with your child.

Day 5:

Teach Emotional Awareness

- Help your child identify and label their emotions.
- Use books and games to explain different feelings.
- Model appropriate emotional responses.

Day 6:

Encourage Independence

- Assign age-appropriate chores and responsibilities.
- Teach problem-solving skills.
- Praise efforts and successes.

Day 7:

Reflect and Adjust

- Review the first week's progress.
- Discuss with your child what's working and what's not.
- Make necessary adjustments to routines and strategies.

Day 8:

Focus on Quality Time

- Plan a special one-on-one activity with your child.
- Make it a screen-free time.
- Listen and engage fully in the activity.

Day 9:

Foster Trust and Respect

- Show respect for your child's opinions and feelings.
- Encourage honesty by being honest yourself.
- Build a foundation of mutual trust.

Day 10:

Positive Discipline Techniques

- Learn about different positive discipline methods.
- Implement time-ins instead of time-outs.
- Use natural consequences to teach responsibility.

Day 11:

Support Academic Growth

- Create a homework-friendly environment.
- Set specific times for study and breaks.
- Celebrate academic achievements, no matter how small.

Day 12:

Promote Healthy Habits

- Teach the importance of a balanced diet.
- Encourage physical activity through family exercises or outdoor play.
- Discuss the benefits of a healthy lifestyle.

Day 13:

Address Behavioral Issues

- Identify any recurring behavioral problems.
- Develop a plan with your child to address these issues.
- Use consistent and calm responses to negative behavior.

Day 14:

Reflect and Adjust

- Review the second week's progress.
- Discuss with your child what's working and what's not.
- Make necessary adjustments to routines and strategies.

Day 15:

Practice Empathy

- Teach your child to understand and share the feelings of others.
- Role-play different scenarios to develop empathy skills.
- Praise empathetic behavior.

Day 16:

Develop Coping Skills
- Teach techniques such as deep breathing, counting to ten, or using a stress ball.
- Practice these techniques during calm moments.
- Encourage your child to use them in stressful situations.

Day 17:

Promote Self-Esteem
- Provide specific praise that focuses on effort, not just results.
- Encourage your child to set and achieve small goals.
- Discuss their strengths and talents.

Day 18:

Teach Conflict Resolution

- Role-play conflict scenarios and possible resolutions.
- Encourage your child to use "I" statements to express feelings.
- Model calm and respectful conflict resolution.

Day 19:

Encourage Social Skills

- Arrange playdates or group activities.
- Teach the importance of sharing and taking turns.
- Discuss the value of friendships.

Day 20:

: Focus on Gratitude

- Start a daily gratitude journal with your child.
- Share things you are both grateful for each day.
- Discuss how gratitude can improve mood and outlook.

Day 21:

Reflect and Adjust

- Review the third week's progress.
- Discuss with your child what's working and what's not.
- Make necessary adjustments to routines and strategies.

Day 22:

Plan Family Activities

- Schedule a weekly family game night or outing.
- Choose activities that everyone enjoys.
- Focus on fun and togetherness.

Day 23:

Encourage Family Meals

- Make family meals a regular event.
- Use this time to connect and communicate.
- Encourage everyone to share their day.

Day 24:

Teach Responsibility

- Assign family chores and responsibilities.
- Use a chore chart to track progress.
- Praise efforts and completion of tasks.

Day 25:

Nurture Individual Interests

- Encourage your child to pursue hobbies and interests.
- Provide resources and support for their passions.
- Celebrate their achievements in these areas.

Day 26:

Practice Mindfulness Together

- Introduce simple mindfulness exercises.
- Practice together daily, even if for a few minutes.
- Discuss how mindfulness can help manage stress

Day 27:

Support Social Connections

- Encourage your child to maintain friendships.
- Discuss the importance of positive peer relationships.
- Help them navigate social challenges.

Day 28:

Strengthen Family Values

- Discuss the core values that are important to your family.
- Model these values in your daily actions.
- Encourage your child to embody these values.

Day 29:

Create a Family Vision Board

- Gather materials to create a vision board together.
- Include goals, dreams, and positive affirmations.
- Display it prominently and review it regularly.

Day 30:

Reflect and Celebrate

- Review the entire month's progress.
- Celebrate the achievements and growth you and your child have made.
- Plan how to continue these positive changes moving forward.